Whales

Children's Nature Library

GALLERY BOOKS
An Imprint of W. H. Smith Publishers Inc

Printed in U.S.A.

8 7 6 5 4 3 2 1

ISBN 0-8317-6464-3

This edition published in 1991 by Gallery Books,
an imprint of W. H. Smith Publishers, Inc.,
112 Madison Avenue, New York, New York 10016.

Gallery Books are available for bulk purchase
for sales and promotions and premium use.
For details write or telephone the Manager of
Special Sales, W. H. Smith Publishers, Inc.,
112 Madison Avenue, New York 10016;
(212) 532-6600.

Written by Eileen Spinelli

Credits:
Animals/Animals: 12; Henry Ausloos: 42, 44;
M.A. Chappel: 17; Ken Cole: 16; E.R. Deg-
ginger: 54, 55; Richard Kolar: 3, 8, 12, 13, 14,
24, 42, 47, 50; Zig Leszczynski: 60; Ted Levin:
20; Oxford Scientific Films/Tony Allen: 6, 7;
Oxford Scientific Films/Tony Martin: 6, 43;
LLT Rhodes: 37, 40; Michael Sacca: 54; John
Stern: 22, 31, 44; J.C. Stevenson: 16; Lewis
Trusty: 48; James D. Watt: 11, 24, 26, 33, 48;
Fred Whitehead: 30; **Nancy A. Butler:** 14;
M.D. Conlin: 20, 46; **Ellis Wildlife Collection:**
Gerry Ellis: Front Cover, 1, 25, 27, 28, 34, 39;
Michael Osmond: 23, 26, 32, 35, 36; **Clayton
Fogle:** 61; **Pieter Folkens:** 9, 10, 18, 19, 22,
28, 29; **FPG International:** Michael S. Kass:
60; Lee Kuhn: 4; **Marine World Africa USA:**
40; Darryl W. Bush: 41; **Flip Nicklin/Nicklin
& Associates:** 58, 59, 62, 63; Oxford Scientific
Films: 62; **Pacific Whale Foundation:** 5, 52,
53, 64, Back Cover; **Sea Squirt Photo:** Warren
D. Barrett: 18, 30, 50; ©**1990 Sea World, Inc.**
Reproduced by permission. All rights reserved.:
Jerry Roberts: 38, 45, 51; **Marty Snyderman:**
15, 21, 36, 56, 57; **Norbert Wu:** 49.

Table of Contents

History of Whales

Millions of years ago, the creature we call a whale was a land animal. It breathed air. It walked around on four legs. It was probably covered with fur and may have looked a lot like a dog.

These whale ancestors lived near the ocean. They probably fed on tiny crabs and fish. At first, the ancestors of the whale may have hunted in shallow water. Later, they went deeper into the sea. They might have used their tails to propel themselves through the water.

History of Whales

With each generation, these whale ancestors began to feel more at home in the ocean than on land. The whale, as we know it today, came into being.

Whales have been hunted since the time of Stone Age people. In early times, small boats were used. Later, larger boats with big white sails went out in search of whales. By the middle of the 1800s, the Americans had 729 ships to hunt whales. Whaling had become a booming industry.

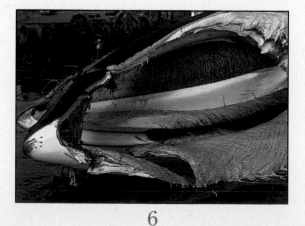

History of Whales

By this time, whales were killed more for their oil and baleen (buh-LEEN) than for their meat. Hairbrushes, whip handles, and fashionable hoops for ladies' dresses were all made from whale baleen, or whalebone.

When steamships were invented, whales that had been too fast for sailing ships could now be caught and killed.

The unhappy result was that by the middle of the 20th century, whale populations were very low. Today, efforts are being made to save the whale.

Where Whales Live

Whales can be found in all the oceans of the world. Some live in lagoons, and a few types live in rivers. Narwhals (NAYR-waylz) spend all year in the cold Arctic Sea. The blue whale is seldom found anywhere but Antarctica.

Some whales live in water so deep that they are rarely seen. Others are seen often, since they live close to shore.

Where Whales Live

Most whales *migrate*. This means that they move from one place to another during different times of the year. There is much more food for whales in the icy waters near the North and South Poles than in the warm, tropical oceans. Whales feed in the cold waters part of the year. Then they travel to warmer seas to have their babies.

How Whales Breathe

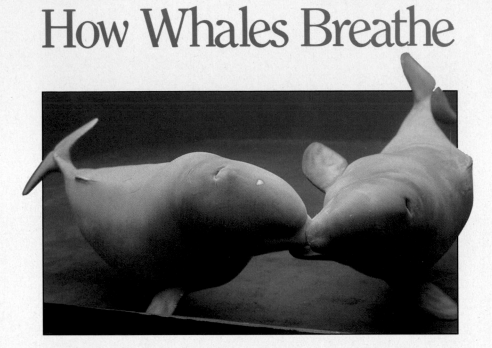

Whales breathe air just like people do. In fact, if a
whale does not come to the surface from time to
time in order to breathe, it will drown. Most whales
can stay underwater for only a short time.
The sperm whale and the bottleneck
whale, however, can stay
underwater for over an hour.
On top of their heads,
whales have odd breathing
devices called blowholes.

How Whales Breathe

When a whale dives underwater, it takes a deep breath. When it comes up out of the water, it exhales, or "blows." Air rushes out of the blowhole in a great, whooshing spout. Experts can tell what kind of whale they have sighted by the height and shape of the spout. Right whales make V-shaped spouts, while the spout of a blue whale is shaped more like an ice-cream cone.

What Whales Eat

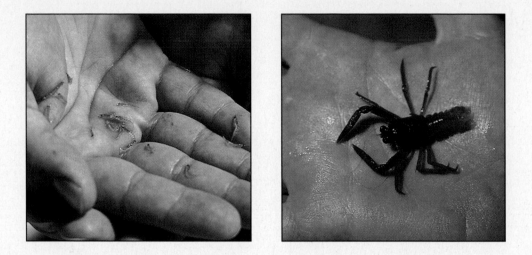

Baleen (buh-LEEN) whales have no teeth. They have baleen plates, which look like the frayed bristles of a giant hairbrush. Baleen is made of the same material as your fingernails. When a baleen whale eats, it slurps huge, watery mouthfuls. It forces the water out between the baleen in its mouth and swallows the food that remains. These whales migrate to the Antarctic to eat tiny, shrimplike creatures called krill.

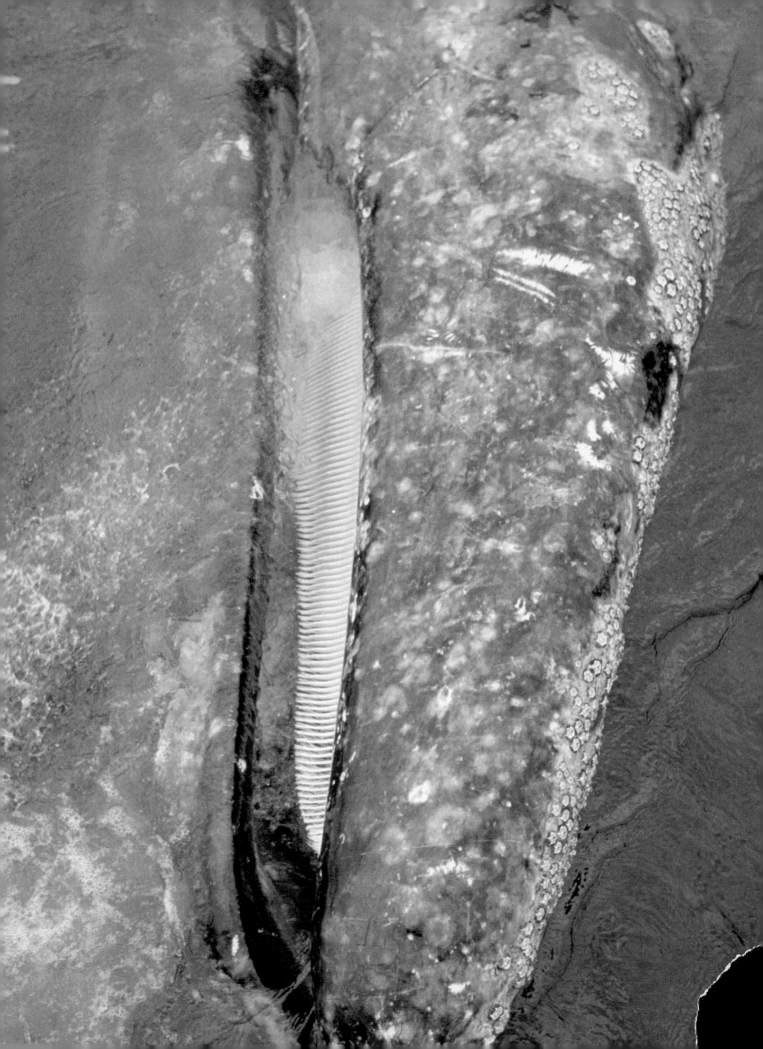

What Whales Eat

Baleen whales also eat small fish such as herring and sardines. They can eat more than a ton of food in one day.

Toothed whales have sharp, pointed teeth. They feed mainly on fish. They also like lobster, starfish, and octopus. One type of toothed whale, called the sperm whale, eats fish and crabs. Its favorite dish, however, is the giant squid.

How Whales Eat

Not all whales eat in the same way. Some feed close to the surface of the water, while others feed in deeper water. Some whales even take their meals at the bottom of the sea.

The killer whale, for example, hunts for food in groups called pods. Another type of whale, called the sperm whale, prefers to dine alone.

Whales have different ways of obtaining food. Some use echoes of their own voices to locate their lunch. Others trap their prey in a circle of bubbles, and eat it with their big, hungry mouths wide open.

In winter, when whales travel to warmer waters to find food, they don't even eat. They have so much stored fat that when they arrive at their summer homes they are still healthy and strong.

How Whales Swim

Whales are excellent swimmers. They move gracefully through the water. Their powerful tails, called flukes, push up and down, propelling them along. Whales prefer to slow-poke at four miles an hour, even though they can swim fast—especially if they are being chased by a hungry shark.

Some whales use their dorsal, or back, fins to keep them steady.

How Whales Swim

A whale does not have to support its own heavy body—the water supports it. If it wants to steer, it just uses its flippers.

Most whales are excellent divers. Certain types of deep-diving whales can plunge up to 3,600 feet below the surface of the water.

Whales don't have to worry about catching cold. A thick layer of fat, called blubber, keeps them warm even in the icy waters of the polar region.

Other Whale Behavior

While some whales swim alone, many travel in groups called pods. Whales in pods often touch each other with their flippers. They have very sensitive skin and clearly enjoy being stroked.

Whales seem to care about each other. They often play and splash together. They also help other whales in trouble and protect their young. Even when they are far apart, some whales send messages to their friends through the water.

Other Whale Behavior

Whales need very little sleep. If a whale falls asleep underwater, the nap will be short—it has to come up to the surface to breathe. Whales sometimes sleep with one eye open. When whales travel in pods, they take turns sleeping. This way, one of them is always awake to keep watch against dangerous enemies. Another interesting fact about sleeping whales is that they snore!

For reasons scientists don't understand, some whales get themselves into trouble. Sometimes, whales follow one another into shallow waters. Then, when the tide goes out, they are "stranded" on the beach. Even when people try to rescue stranded whales by setting them afloat, they return to land. Stranded whales usually die.

Language of the Whale

Whale "talk" is being studied by scientists. Some whales "speak" in clicks, chirps, and whistles. Others groan, grunt, and moan. The humpback whale sings. A recording of its song was even carried into space by the spaceship *Voyager*.

Whales call to one another near and far. They cry to alert friends if they see danger. They also navigate to the sound of their own echoes.

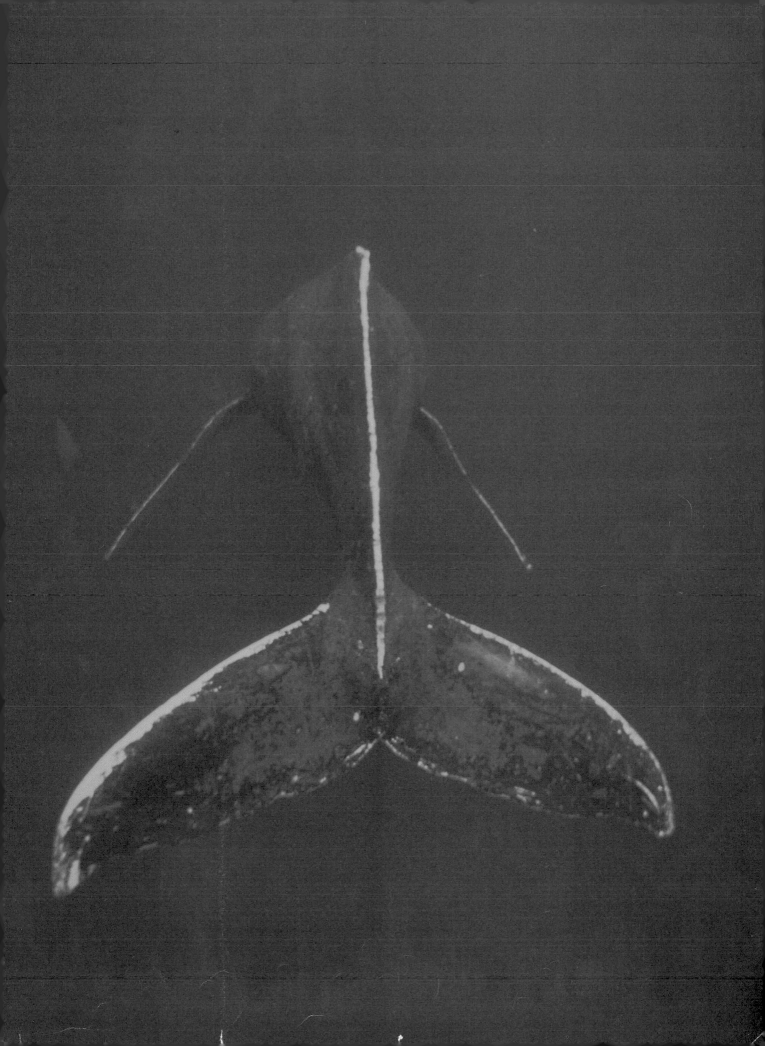

Language of the Whale

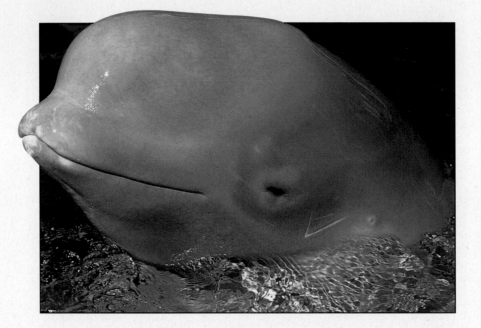

Whales hear very well, even though their ears are very small. They are nothing more than small holes in the surface of their bodies.

Many whale sounds can be heard by humans. If a blue whale or a sperm whale ever "spoke" to you, you probably would want to hold your ears. These creatures have very loud voices.

Like humans, whales also use the language of touch to express themselves and to show affection.

Mothers & Babies

When a mother whale is ready to give birth, she often invites a friend to help her. A whale baby is born underwater, tailfirst. Its eyes are open and it is ready to swim. A baby whale must get to the surface of the water immediately, since it needs air to breathe right away. Some babies can get to the surface with no help at all. Others need a nudge from their mother or her friend.

Mothers & Babies

Like puppies and kittens, baby whales feed on milk from their mothers' bodies. Since a baby whale cannot stay underwater very long, it needs to nurse quickly. Mother sometimes helps it along by squirting milk into her baby's mouth. Baby whales are curious and playful. They nose up to boats and floating driftwood. They also ride the waves.

Mother whales are very affectionate and caring. They stroke their babies, hold them on their bellies, and pat them with their flippers. During the first year of a baby's life, a mother whale will not let it stray from her side. Mother whale continues to protect her young years after it is born. If her baby is threatened, a mother whale becomes angry and dangerous.

In Captivity

A large whale cannot be kept in captivity. It eats too much and is too big to be kept in a pool. Smaller whales are kept instead. Although fierce and terrifying at sea, killer whales are playful, obedient, and easily tamed in captivity.

Whales in oceanariums put on delightful shows. Oceanariums are not just for fun, however. They also give scientists a chance to study these amazing creatures.

Save The Whale

Since early times, whales have been hunted and killed. Less than a century ago, 200,000 blue whales were believed to be living in the Antarctic. Today, the blue whale is quite rare. The gray whale was hunted right out of the Atlantic Ocean. Fortunately, this whale reappeared along the Pacific coast.

Today, there are strict laws to protect the whale. These laws are very important.

Killer Whale

The killer whale is fearsome and fast. It hunts in groups called pods and will attack seals, walruses, squid, sea turtles, and even other whales. It will gulp down anything it can get its teeth into. With its shiny black-and-white coat, the killer whale looks a bit like a penguin. In captivity, the killer whale is friendly and full of fun.

Blue Whale

Imagine three or four dinosaurs—that's how heavy a blue whale is! Its heart is the size of a small car. Its tongue weighs as much as an elephant. The blue whale eats four tons of food a day. When it moans, get out your earplugs—it sounds louder than a jet engine. Yet, the blue whale is quite graceful. It lives in small family groups and is one of the rarest whales.

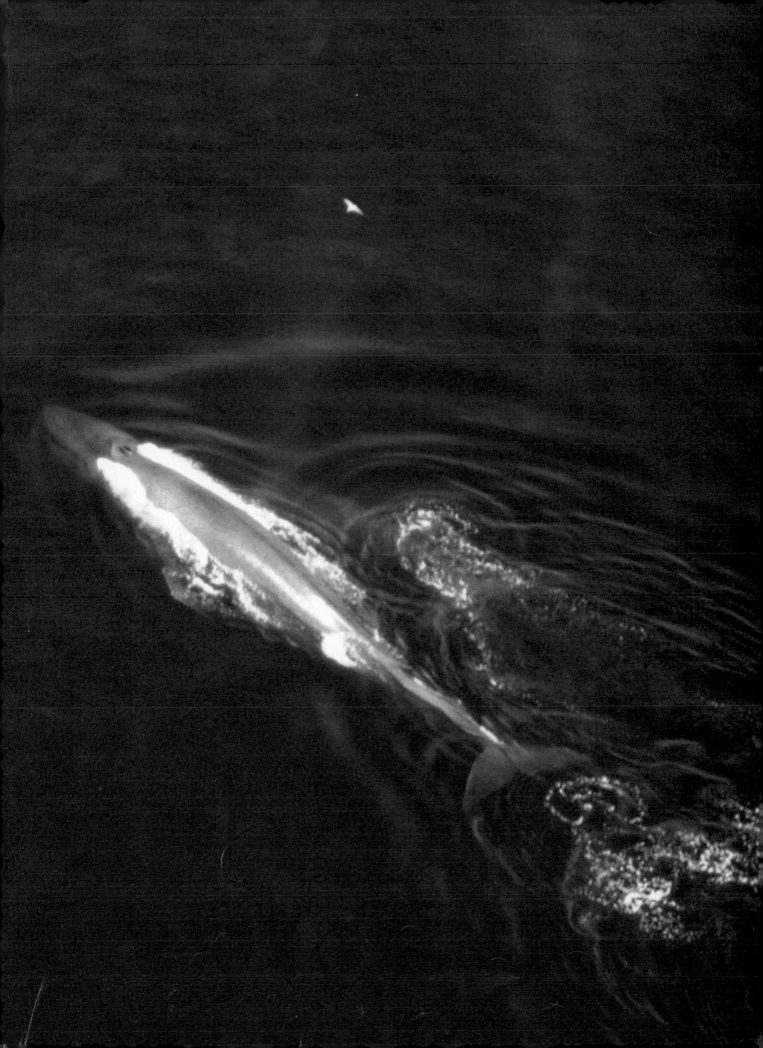

Pilot Whale

The pilot whale has a bulging forehead. Its head looks like a big, upside-down soup pot. It is sometimes called the "pothead" whale. These whales live in pods or groups of several hundred. Like geese, they travel in formation and follow a leader.

Fishermen used to follow pilot whales to lead them to schools of fish. The pilot whale is smart. In addition, it is one of the most commonly sighted whales.

Gray Whale

The gray whale's summer home in the northern Pacific is very far from its winter home along the coast of Baja California. When the gray whale travels, it seldom stops to rest or eat. When it is not traveling, the gray whale eats quite a lot. It scrapes its way across the bottom of the ocean, feeding on small fish and tiny sea creatures. Eating this way scars the gray whale's head.

Humpback Whale

Male humpback whales sing! The songs of this musical whale are strange, haunting, and beautiful. Over time, the songs seem to change.

The humpback whale is a wonderfully acrobatic whale, too. It leaps straight out of the sea, and it swims playfully on its back. To attract the attention of the female, the male humpback tries to stand on its head in the water.

Fin Whale

Because of its speed and grace, the fin whale is often called the "greyhound of the sea." Next to the blue whale, it is the largest animal in the world. Its lower jaw is black on one side and white on the other. It also sports a beard. Fin whales take huge mouthfuls and gulp their food. This whale swims in all the world's oceans.

Great Right Whale

Great right whales are slow swimmers. They are also curious, often coming close to boats. To hunters, they were the "right" whale to catch. The great right whale performs an exciting trick called "breaching." It propels its body out of the sea high into the air. Then, it crashes down with a thunderous SPLASH! The great right whale is amazingly flexible. It can almost touch its head to its tail.

Sperm Whale

The largest nose in the world belongs to the sperm whale. This whale weighs up to 12 tons! The sperm whale also has the largest brain of any animal on earth. This whale's favorite food is giant squid. Catching its supper, however, is no easy task. The giant squid, like any sensible creature, puts up a terrific fight—there are round scars on many sperm whales to prove it.

Beluga Whale

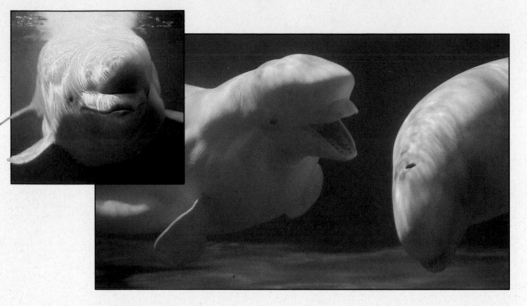

Newborn belugas (buh-LOO-guhz) are gray. Adults are white. Their coats blend in with the ice and snow of their arctic home. The beluga swims beneath the ice and comes up to breathe through any holes. When a beluga gets trapped under the ice, it will ram through the ice with its head. OUCH! In summer, beluga whales may travel up rivers. They make whistling, chirping sounds. Sailors used to call them "sea canaries."

Narwhal

No one seems to be able to figure out why the male narwhal (NAYR-wayl) has a long horn, which is really an extra-long tooth. Some believe it's used to poke holes in the thick polar ice. Others think narwhals use it as a fencing sword. Some even think that this tooth helps to carry the narwhal's sounds. Narwhals live in deep water in winter. In summer, they swim closer to the shore.